A to Z The Dominican Republic

BY BYRON AUGUSTIN

children's press®

A Division of Scholastic Inc.
New York Toronto London Auckland Sydney
Mexico City New Delhi Hong Kong
Danbury, Connecticut

Consultant: Dr. Aldo Lauria-Santiago, Professor, College of the Holy Cross, Worcester, Massachusetts
Series Design: Marie O'Neill
Photo Research: Caroline Anderson
Language Consultant: Dr. Aldo Lauria-Santia

The photos on the cover show a parrot fish (top left), Fort San Felipe (top right),
two Dominican Republic boys (bottom right), and a spider trapped in amber (bottom center).

Photographs © 2005: Alamy Images/PCL: 34 bottom, 37 bottom; AP/Wide World Photos: 28 bottom (Rick Bowmer), 14 (Alden Pellett), 15 right (Suzanne Plunkett); Bruce Coleman Inc.: 12 top (M. Timothy O'Keefe), 36 (Sullivan & Rogers); Byron Augustin: 22; Corbis Images: 9 right, 15 left, 31 (Tony Arruza), 38 (Reinhard Eisele), 29 (Macduff Everton), cover center right, cover bottom center, 6 left, 7, 10, 16 (Franz-Marc Frei), 4 (Stephen Frink), 25 (Jeremy Horner), 5 top (David Hosking/Frank Lane Picture Agency), 27 right (Catherine Karnow), 8 (Danny Lehman), 21 (Giraud Philippe/Sgyma), cover top left (Royalty-Free); Envision Stock Photography Inc./Rita Maas: 11; Getty Images/Colin Keates/Dorling Kindersley: cover bottom right; Index Stock Imagery/ Timothy O'Keefe: 28 top; Landov, LLC/John Riley/EPA: 12 bottom; Larimar Museum: 23; Masterfile/Dale Wilson: 18; NHPA/Daniel Heuclin: 5 bottom; Otto Piron: 35 bottom, 37 top; Photo Researchers, NY/J. P. Courau: 32; Superstock, Inc./Stock Montage: 13; The Image Works: 26 (Brett Sussman/V&W), 17 (Topham); Tom Bean: 6 right, 9 left, 19, 24, 27 left, 30, 34 top, 35 top; TRIP Photo Library/Helene Rogers: 33.
Map by XNR Productions, Inc.

Library of Congress Cataloging-in-Publication Data
Augustin, Byron.
  The Dominican Republic / by Byron Augustin.
     p. cm. — (A to Z)
  Includes bibliographical references and index.
  ISBN 0-516-23663-6 (lib. bdg.)   0-516-24951-7 (pbk.)
  1. Dominican Republic—Juvenile literature. I. Title. II. Series.
  F1934.2.A94 2005
  972.93—dc22   2005006996

1 2 3 4 5 6 7 8 9 10 R 14 13 12 11 10 09 08 07 06 05

Contents

Animals

Manatees graze underwater and are nicknamed "sea cows."

The Dominican Republic on the island of Hispaniola does not have large, wild land animals. The country has many small animals and hundreds of birds. Fish, dolphins, whales, and Caribbean manatees swim in the waters surrounding the island.

The Hispaniolan, or cotica, parrot is known for its brilliant green feathers and talkative nature.

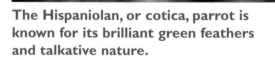

A shy hutia

The hutia is a small **rodent** and is very shy. It lives in the forests and comes out at night to eat. The hutia was an important part of the native diet and may have been the first meat that Christopher Columbus tasted in the **New World.**

Solendons are clumsy animals with long noses. They have sharp claws that they use to dig for worms and snails. If they move too fast, they sometimes trip over their own feet!

The cotica parrot is the national bird of the Dominican Republic. Its feathers are bright green. It is a noisy bird that loves to talk and squawk. Because it is **endangered**, it is now protected.

Fort San Felipe

A guard stands watch in front of what is believed to be the tomb of Christopher Columbus.

Buildings

There are many old buildings in the Dominican Republic. Fort San Felipe is more than 450 years old. Its walls are 8 feet (2.4 meters) thick.

The Faro de Colón (Columbus Lighthouse) is a new building. It was built in 1992 to mark the 500-year anniversary of Christopher Columbus landing in the Americas. Inside, there is a large marble tomb. Many Dominicans believe the tomb contains the bones of Columbus.

Faro

(FA-roe)
means "lighthouse"
in Spanish.

Puerto Plata

(PWAIR-toe PLA-ta)
means "silver port"
in Spanish.

One of Puerto Plata's loveliest parks

Cities

Santo Domingo is the oldest European city in the Americas. It is also the country's capital. The city has almost 3 million residents. There are many old colonial buildings.

Santiago and Puerto Plata are also important cities. Santiago is the second-largest city. It is famous as the major industrial center in the Dominican Republic. Puerto Plata is a port and tourist center.

Cool, colorful clothing is just right
for the Dominican Republic.

Dress

Most Dominicans wear modern clothes
made from cotton. Cotton cloth is best
for the country's warm, humid weather.

Many business executives prefer a casual look.

Kids just like to be comfortable!

Most Dominicans prefer casual, comfortable clothing. Loose-fitting shirts and blouses are the choice of many adults. Children wear shorts and T-shirts, along with sandals or sports shoes. In rural areas, children often go barefoot.

Professionals and businesspeople usually wear suits. For special occasions, women may choose long dresses in bright colors such as yellow, orange, and red. Matching jewelry, including bracelets, necklaces, and earrings, is also popular.

Sugarcane harvest

Exports

There are many farms and plantations in the Dominican Republic. Farmers grow sugarcane, coffee, cotton, **cacao,** rice, beans, and corn. Sugar is the most important agricultural export.

The country's workers also mine **nickel** and gold for export. Textile and clothing factories employ thousands of workers. The United States is the country's major trade partner.

CORN FLOUR FRITTERS

WHAT YOU NEED:

- 1 cup of corn flour
- 2 tablespoons of milk
- 1 teaspoon of sugar
- 1/2 teaspoon of salt
- 1 egg
- 1/4 cup of oil

HOW TO MAKE IT:

Mix all of the ingredients, except the oil, in a mixing bowl. Stir well. Heat the oil in a shallow frying pan. Pour the mix one tablespoon at a time into the hot oil. Each spoonful will make one small cake. Fry the cakes until they are golden brown on both sides. Remove from the frying pan and serve hot.

Food

Corn flour fritters are a popular snack in the Dominican Republic. They can be made in fifteen minutes. Ask an adult to help you make the recipe above.

The National Palace in Santo Domingo

Government

The government of the Dominican Republic is a **representative democracy**. All citizens over eighteen years of age, except the police, members of the military, and prisoners, may vote in elections. The president is elected to a four-year term and may be reelected many times.

A **dictator** named General Rafael Trujillo ruled the country from 1930 to 1961. He was a ruthless man who tortured and murdered many of his opponents. Trujillo was also a **racist**. In 1937, he ordered the killing of up to twenty thousand black Dominicans mostly of Hatian descent.

The country's current leader, Leonel Fernandez Reyna, has been president since 1996 and was reelected to his third four-year term in 2004.

President Leonel Fernandez Reyna

History

Christopher Columbus and his men landing on Hispaniola

The Spanish were the first Europeans on the island of Hispaniola. After conquering the native population, Spain started the first European colony in the Americas. The Spanish built churches, hospitals, and a university. They planted sugarcane in large fields. They also brought black slaves from Africa to work in the fields and in mines.

The French also established a colony on the island. This colony grew into the nation of Haiti. Today, the Dominican Republic and Haiti share Hispaniola.

Important People

The Dominican Republic has given the
world many creative people. Two of the
most famous are Julia Alvarez and Oscar
de la Renta.

The beautiful Casa de Campo resort

**Oscar de la Renta,
with a model wearing
one of his gowns**

Julia Alvarez is a beloved storyteller and poet. When she was a child, her family fled the Dominican Republic to escape General Trujillo. Her most famous book, *In the Time of the Butterflies*, tells the true story of three sisters who were killed for resisting Trujillo.

Oscar de la Renta is a famous fashion designer. Men and women all over the world wear clothing he has designed. He also helped design Casa de Campo, a beautiful tourist resort in the Dominican Republic.

Salt miners hard at work

Jobs

More than half of all Dominicans work in service jobs. They are teachers, nurses, and government workers. They also work in the tourist industry to help visitors feel welcome.

Other citizens work in mines and on farms. Some workers specialize in making jewelry from native stones. Many women work in clothing factories. Often, Dominicans leave their country to find better jobs in the United States or Puerto Rico, but they always return to visit friends and relatives.

Keepsakes

Much of the world's amber is found in the Dominican Republic. Amber is formed when **resin** oozes from trees and is buried underground or underwater. After millions of years, the resin turns to soft stone. Insects trapped inside the sticky resin are sometimes found in the amber.

Amber is made into beautiful jewelry by the Dominicans. Amber is one of the few stones that will float in water.

Amber jewelry from the Dominican Republic is prized around the world.

The golden sands and turquoise waters of a typical Dominican Republic beach

Land

Mountains cover almost 80 percent of the Dominican Republic. Golden, sandy beaches are found along the country's coast.

Inland from the beaches, the Dominican Republic is mostly mountainous.

There are three major mountain ranges in the Dominican Republic. The highest peaks reach above 10,000 feet (3,050 m). In the winter, snow can be seen on these high peaks. Rich farmland is found in the mountain valleys.

Many of the best beaches are along the north coast near Puerto Plata. Thousands of tourists visit these beaches to soak up the sun.

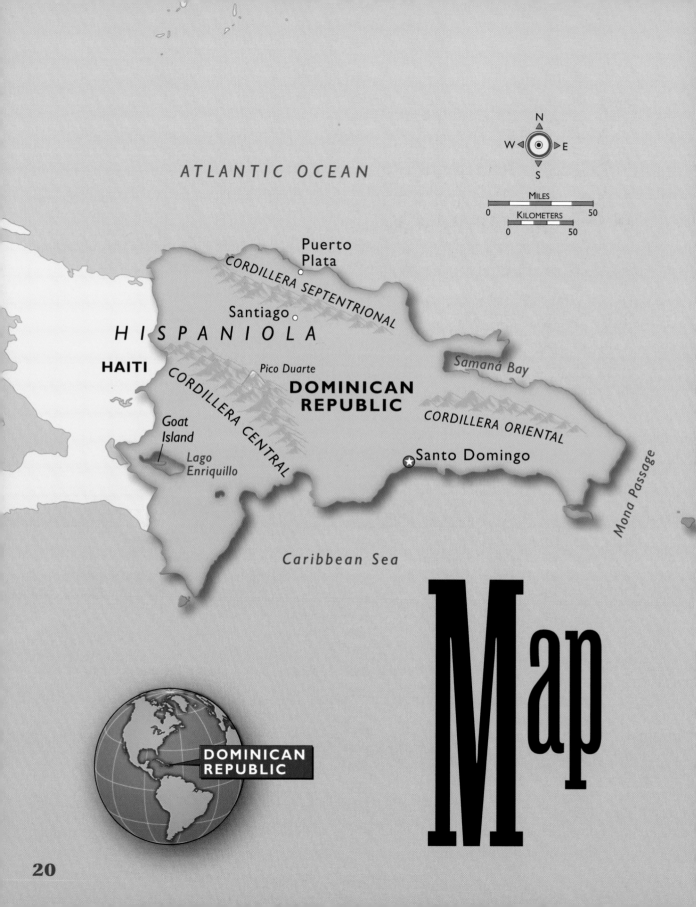

ATLANTIC OCEAN

N
W ◄◉► E
S

MILES
0   50

KILOMETERS
0   50

Puerto
Plata

CORDILLERA SEPTENTRIONAL

Santiago

HISPANIOLA

HAITI

CORDILLERA CENTRAL

Pico Duarte

DOMINICAN
REPUBLIC

Samaná Bay

CORDILLERA ORIENTAL

Goat
Island

Lago
Enriquillo

Santo Domingo

Mona Passage

Caribbean Sea

DOMINICAN
REPUBLIC

Map

Nation

The flag of the Dominican Republic was officially adopted in 1844. The design includes four rectangles of equal size. Two of the rectangles are blue and represent liberty. Two are red and represent the blood spilled for independence.

A white cross is located in the center of the flag and separates the colored rectangles. The cross represents the Catholic faith. The nation's coat of arms is found in the center of the cross.

This raw larimar was found deep in a volcano and is ready to be made into jewelry.

Only in the Dominican Republic

Larimar is a very rare **gemstone**. It is mined from a single mountain in the Dominican Republic and cannot be found anywhere else in the world.

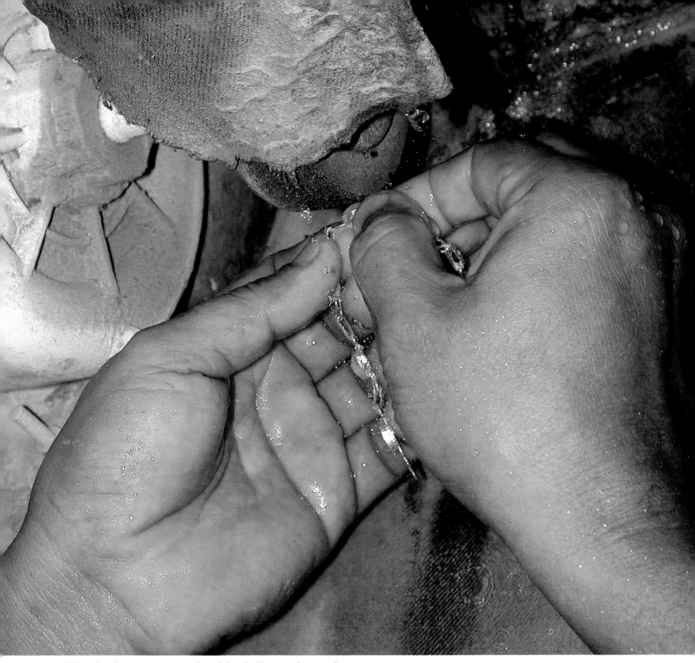

The larimar stones in this delicate bracelet
match the waters of the Caribbean Sea.

Larimar is formed inside a volcano. Miners dig deep holes
into the volcano in search of this rare stone.

Larimar comes in beautiful shades of blue, like the waters
of the Caribbean Sea. Jewelers make earrings, pendants, and
necklaces from larimar.

Most Dominicans today have Spanish and African ancestors.

People

The Native Americans of the Dominican Republic are gone. They died hundreds of years ago, from abuse by the island's Spanish conquerors and from European diseases. Today, most Dominicans have **ancestors** who came from Spain and Africa.

Many houses are painted bright, cheerful colors and have metal roofs.

Dominican families are usually large. They love to celebrate birthdays, anniversaries, and holidays together.

In rural areas, people mostly live in small wooden houses with metal roofs. The houses are painted in bright colors such as blue, pink, green, and yellow.

In the cities, wealthy families live in large **mansions** and luxury apartments. Less well-to-do people live in concrete houses with stucco walls and small garages. The poorest Dominicans live in **slums**. Their houses are flimsy shacks without running water or electricity.

Humpback whale

Question Why do humpback whales visit the Dominican Republic?

Several thousand humpback whales visit the Dominican Republic each winter. They swim more than 3,100 miles (5,000 kilometers) from the Arctic Ocean. They spend the winter months in Samaná Bay on the northeast coast.

Mother humpback whales have their babies in the warm tropical water. A baby whale is called a calf. Humpback calves are about 14 feet long (4.3 m) and weigh up to 5,000 pounds (2,300 kilograms). A baby humpback can drink 100 pounds (50 kg) of milk each day.

Religion

Inside the Cathedral of Santa María la Menor

Almost all Dominicans are members of the Roman Catholic Church. They celebrate religious holidays such as Christmas, Good Friday, Easter, and All Soul's Day.

The oldest Catholic cathedral in the New World is located in Santo Domingo. The Cathedral of Santa María la Menor was built between 1514 and 1546. The front of the cathedral is made from **coral** rock.

Inside the cathedral, there are many small chapels. Until 1992, when the Faro de Colón was built, bones believed to be those of Christopher Columbus were kept in one of the chapels.

A happy schoolgirl

Béisbol

(BAYS-bowl)
means "baseball"
in Spanish.

School & Sports

Children between the ages of five and fourteen are required to attend school. In rural areas, some children quit school to earn money for their families. Only a small number of children go to high school or college.

Baseball is the most popular sport in the Dominican Republic. Many Dominican baseball players come to the United States to play professional baseball. Sammy Sosa, formerly of the Chicago Cubs and now with the Baltimore Orioles, is one of the most popular Dominican players.

Sammy Sosa is famous for his home runs.

This colorful bus has a thatched roof.

Transportation

In general, roads in the Dominican Republic are of poor quality. Less than half of the roads are paved. Most people ride buses that are slow and uncomfortable.

Santo Domingo and Puerto Plata are the major ports in the Dominican Republic. Ships bring grain and other products to the ports. The country has a major naval base in Santo Domingo.

Lago Enriquillo is the largest lake in the Dominican Republic.

Unusual Places

Lago
(LA-goh)
means "lake"
in Spanish.

El Parque Los Tres Ojos (The Park of Three Eyes) is a special attraction. The "three eyes" are lakes in caves connected by an underground river. The first lake has **sulfur** water. The second lake has very cold water. The third lake is shallow and warm.

Lago Enriquillo is the largest lake in the Dominican Republic. The lake is located 130 feet (40 m) below sea level. Goat Island is a popular tourist attraction in the lake. American crocodiles that grow up to 15 feet (4.6 m) long live on the island.

El Limon Waterfall is one of the most dramatic and beautiful spots in the Dominican Republic.

Visiting the Country

Thousands of tourists visit the Dominican Republic each year. Some walk along beautiful sandy beaches. Some swim and **snorkel** in the aqua blue waters of the ocean. Others hike in the mountains to observe waterfalls in quiet **rain forests**.

Luxury hotels attract people who enjoy gambling in casinos. Guests eat delicious food in five-star restaurants. The hotels also provide beautiful swimming pools located in tropical gardens.

Christopher Columbus's three ships were the *Niña*, the *Pinta*, and the *Santa María*.

Window to the Past

Christopher Columbus was the first European to set foot in the Dominican Republic. He arrived in 1492.

Stone sculpture of Christopher Columbus and Queen Isabel of Castille

Columbus wanted to find a trade route from Europe to Asia by crossing the Atlantic Ocean. He asked Queen Isabel of Castille, in Spain, for money to pay for his search. But instead of finding India and China, Columbus reached the Americas.

Christopher Columbus and his crew sailed to the Americas on three boats. These boats were named the *Niña*, the *Pinta*, and the *Santa María*.

X-tra Special Things

Carnaval masks are colorful.

Diablo

(dee AB low) means "devil" in Spanish.

Paraders wearing diablo costumes during Carnaval

Making a diablo, or devil, mask

Devil masks worn during the celebration of Carnaval are very popular in the Dominican Republic. The masks represent the fight between good and evil.

Some of the most elaborate devil masks are made in the towns of Santiago and La Vega. Some masks are playful and represent popular characters such as the "Beggar Woman." Other masks are very scary and represent the "Devil" or "Evil One."

The masks are usually made from clay or papier-mâché and are painted in bright colors. Almost all masks have long horns. Children love to chase the "devils" during parades.

Everyone loves a parade!

Yearly Festivals

The most popular festival in the Dominican Republic is Carnaval. This festival is celebrated before **Lent**.

During Carnaval, there are lots of parades. People dress in bright costumes. They dance in the streets to loud music.

El Malecon glitters with lights at night.

Dominicans celebrate New Year's Eve on El Malecon. El Malecon is a wide street along the ocean in Santo Domingo. There are bands, food booths, and a fireworks show. People dance to joyful music called merengue.

Another person at Carnaval

Alcazar de Colón

Zona Colonial

The Zona Colonial in Santo Domingo is one of the most important historical districts in the Americas. It contains the oldest street, oldest cathedral, and oldest military building in the New World.

The Alcazar de Colón is a beautiful local palace. It has twenty-two rooms, and its walls are more than 3 feet (1 m) thick. The Alcazar was built around 1515 by Christopher Columbus's son, Diego Colón. Diego was governor of the island during its first years under Spanish rule.

■ Spanish and English Words

ancestors the people from whom a person is descended; your grandparents are your ancestors

cacao a plant that produces a seed used to make chocolate

coral the hardened skeletons of sea animals

endangered a species or a type of animal or plant that is in danger of becoming extinct

dictator a person who rules a country without sharing power

gemstone a precious stone that can be cut and polished

Lent the forty days before Easter during which many Catholics give up meat and other pleasures

mansions large, beautiful homes built by wealthy people

New World the land of North and South America, which was settled by European nations

nickel a metal ore used to make steel strong

racist a person who believes that one race (usually his or her own) is superior to another race

rain forests areas of thick, tropical trees that receive heavy rainfall

representative democracy a type of government in which the citizens of a nation elect their leaders

resin a sticky substance that seeps out of certain trees

rodent animals with two big front teeth used for gnawing

slums crowded areas with poor housing and dirty living conditions

snorkel to swim with a breathing tube and a mask, allowing a person to look and breathe underwater

sulfur a chemical element used in fertilizer and explosives; it has a bad odor

■ Let's Explore More

Dominican Republic by Elaine Landau, Children's Press, 2000

Sammy Sosa: He's the Man by Laura Driscoll, Disney Press, 1999

The Secret Footprints by Julia Alvarez, Dragonfly Books, 2002

Websites

http://www.dominicancooking.com/dominicanrecipes.htm
This site offers a large number of recipes for typical Dominican foods. Food categories include low-calorie, vegetarian, easy, and fast.

http://www.enchantedlearning.com/languages/spanish/Aisfor.shtml
This site includes a delightful English-Spanish picture dictionary. Each word is printed in both English and Spanish and is accompanied by an appropriate color picture.

Index

Meet the Author

BYRON AUGUSTIN was raised on a farm in Nebraska. He currently lives in New Braunfels, Texas, and is a professor of geography at Texas State University–San Marcos. He received a bachelor's degree from Hastings College, a master's degree from the University of Kansas, and his doctorate from the University of Northern Colorado.

He has visited fifty-four countries on five continents. He is an accomplished photographer with more than 1,150 published photos. His photos have been published by the National Geographic Society, Encyclopedia Britannica, Scholastic, and many other publishers. He is the author of *Qatar, The United Arab Emirates, Bolivia,* and *Panama* in the Enchantment of the World book series.